Wendy's Club

...for women hooked on "Peter Pans" and how to break the addiction

by
Patricia Diane Craine M.A.-L.M.F.T.

Bloomington, IN Milton Keynes, UK
authorHOUSE®

AuthorHouse™
1663 Liberty Drive, Suite 200
Bloomington, IN 47403
www.authorhouse.com
Phone: 1-800-839-8640

AuthorHouse™ UK Ltd.
500 Avebury Boulevard
Central Milton Keynes, MK9 2BE
www.authorhouse.co.uk
Phone: 08001974150

First published by AuthorHouse 9/28/2006

ISBN: 1-4259-6047-2 (sc)

Printed in the United States of America
Bloomington, Indiana

This book is printed on acid-free paper.

Library of Congress Control Number: 2006907767

When you have reached the end of all the light that you know, and you must step out into the darkness of the unknown, Faith is knowing that one of two things will happen: Either you will have something solid to stand on or you will be taught how to fly!

Author unknown

This Book Is Dedicated to all
The Wonderful Wendys,
Past, Present and Future

Introduction

What's a nice girl like me doing in a Clubhouse like this?

She never intended to become a member of the club. Quite to the contrary she was always there helping her friends, who claimed they got caught behind the club's door.

Our Wendy is bright charming and dependable. If you need to get the job done, she's your gal. She is very well liked by others and always there to help lend a helping hand or ear. But she hasn't been very successful at love relationships in the past.

But, one day, she meets a guy we will call "Peter". At first she finds him somewhat immature and is not terribly attracted to him. However, once she's been around him for a while, she finds him intriguing, almost in a "playful, little boy way". He teases her, he makes her laugh. She amazingly finds herself having a good time!

He seems to be really nice and friends around him really seem to enjoy his company. He asks for her phone number.

Wendy thinks to herself, "He really seems like a great guy. He's a lot of fun and a good dancer! Oh why not?" But what Wendy doesn't know is that she is knocking on the Clubhouse door . . .

Table of Contents

Appreciation

With appreciation to the staff at AuthorHouse, particularly, Bob DeGroff and a very special appreciation to Tracie McLean, my agent, my mentor and my friend. Also a special thank you to Janice May and Bob Mullins for their talents in getting Wendy to fly!!!

<u>Acknowledgements</u>

With humbleness and deepest gratitude
to...
My wings...
my mentor and spiritual guide, I call God
My rock...
my angel and precious Grandma Doddie
My anchor...
my forever love, Bud

Author's note

For the purpose of this book I am using the female gender as Wendy. However the concepts are, in reality, gender transferable. The "Wendy/Peter" mode can be any age, any religion, any race, male female, straight or gay. We are all basically the same in regard to our relationship issues.

Patricia Craine

The Creator Of Wendy: The REAL Peter Pan

Peter Pan was written by Sir James Michael Barrie in 1904. It was originally a play about a little boy who refused to grow up, Barrie, the youngest of nine children decided to become a writer to please his mother.

He became very successful from his writing and was always generous with his financial success. Once married, but childless, Barrie later financed a refuge home for women and children.

In 1922, James Barrie was invested with the title Sir, at Buckingham Palace.

He, in later years, donated the rights to Peter Pan to London's Great Ormond Street Hospital for sick children.

Sir Barrie died on June 19, 1937 at the age of seventy-seven. But, of course, in all of our hearts . . . he will NEVER grow old!

Through the Grace of God, if our candle
becomes illuminated, I believe our job
is to pass it forward so the process can
continue, hopefully to generations to
follow. We are all students and teachers
in great classroom we call Life.

Patricia Craine

Prologue

In the past 20 years of my Psychotherapy practice, I have obviously seen many individuals, couples, families and circumstances. They have all come from different walks of life, all various challenges and/or tragedies. All genders, races, financial situations, all ages and stages in their lives – They have all come through the same door.

They all feel "stuck" as in a freeway lane that will not move. My job, as I see it, is to view their situation from my traffic helicopter perspective and move them into a lane that flows for them. I call it "positive problem solving."

Some people, I believe, I have helped move into that diamond lane and they have been able to positively continue on their path. For others, I will never know.

My own personal struggles with dramas, traumas, addictions and compulsions spiritually led me to return to school and obtain my Masters. At 39 years old, I began the long arduous process toward becoming a licensed psychotherapist.

At the beginning of each session I personally share that "98% of what is shared in this room, I have either gone through, am personally going through or someday perhaps will go through." I believe we are all on the same boat of life. No one is any better than anyone else. I also believe the secret of life is balance and also to learn and grow from each and every experience/person we encounter.

We often learn more from the negatives than we do from the positives. The point is, to learn from the lesson and make the choice to grow forward.

In recent years, I began to realize that my practice is no longer the varied population it once was. Today I basically see the same type of female patient. She comes in and out, each day, week and month! Obviously they have different faces, different bodies and personalities. They can be any age or stage, race, gender, straight, gay, single, married, separated or divorced. But the commonalities are always quite amazing. The have striking similarities of family histories, dating histories, self esteem issues and repetitive patterns. Ironically, they all seem to be members of the same club . . . I call it . . . Wendy's Club.

Wendy's First Session

She would be out in public and see all these couples, seemingly so happy and here she was all alone. Her "inner critic" begins.... "Maybe I should lose weight or dye my hair blonde. Am I not cute enough or smart enough? Am I going to be alone forever? What is wrong with me? Why can't I find a great guy who adores me? Other gals don't seem to seem to have this problem." Most (or many) women view "success", as in a relationship. They think, "If I were in a relationship, I would be happy and then I would be more successful in other areas of my life. I would have an identity . . . be part of a couple, not alone." Obviously, this self examination or self deterioration is extremely damaging to one's confidence and self value.

There is also the societal pressure regarding a single woman. "Why doesn't she have a man in her life, etc." Of course, we know, no one really makes our life whole, happy or complete. It is up to us to accomplish this task. But, why is the question asked about the single girl and not the single guy??

Wendy comes in for her first session. She presents well. She tells me she has lots of good friends, has a great job with a boss that really likes her. She describes herself as responsible, dependable and "I'm always there for my friends." She has typically two dogs that were found as strays. She is friendly, warm and sincere. She tells me, despite all the good things in her life, she doesn't have success with love relationships, and doesn't know why. She begins to tear, "My problem is my boyfriend. I do everything for him and he treats me like dirt. But, then he'll be so sweet again, so I stay in the relationship." Wendy tells me that she tends to hesitate with men due to prior painful relationships, but the night she met (she calls him Peter), she started really having a great time! She tells me that prior to Peter she felt really lonely and depressed.

Wendy admits to me she basically has low self esteem. She doesn't feel confident or comfortable going out to bars with her friends. She has dated other guys, some very nice, polite, had good jobs, etc. But they were just <u>boring</u>. Then her last relationship ended after two years. She just finally got "fed up" with his broken promises and her giving 95% into the relationship and him giving 5% (if that). It still stings.

Do you know a Wendy? Does this sound like someone you know – your girlfriend, your sister, your mother, or even . . . yourself? This new Miss Wendy sitting in my office doesn't know it yet . . . but she has just become newest member of <u>Wendy's Club</u>.

Looking Back . . . Wendy

In order to go forward we must learn and understand from the past. It is important for all of us to understand the child within us, one's childhood and our family of origin. The multi-generational transmission process gives us insight and clues to the current behaviors and to the rules and roles of our past and present.

Typically, Wendy is born into a family that on the outside seems fairly "functional/normal" (whatever that is!)

From a young age, much is expected of Wendy. Her mother is not particularly warm or nurturing. That is not to say she is not a good, functional role mother, but just not the warm and fuzzy June Cleaver type. Wendy wants very hard to please her mother. She does what she is told, picks up her toys, has very nice manners and is very pleasant to all she meets. Other mothers love her, children love to play with her and she is always teacher's favorite.

Mother of course expects all this, so Wendy is never really complimented on these characteristics, but she feels if she keeps on doing all her chores, getting good grades and taking responsibility in the family, mom will be very pleased indeed!

Mom wears the pants (even though Dad might not admit it). She often works outside the home and is often involved with a community activity of some sort. She stays very busy. So, often it is Wendy who is taking care of the little ones, cooking dinner, and keeping the house tidied up. (Mom had another obligation late again tonight.)

And then, there's Dad. Dad is warmer to Wendy, but very passive in nature. He acquiesces to Mom's agenda. Looking back Wendy might say he was somewhat lazy, until Mom yelled and nagged at him. Although often employed, he like to watch T.V. in his favorite chair, with a "few beers" then fall asleep. He was not ambitious, but a gentle soul.

So, it was definitely Mom in this household who was the stronger parent and made most of the decisions. Mom expected Wendy's help around the house and expected her to achieve and be responsible in all areas of Wendy's life. Wendy thinks that the higher she achieves, "The happier mom would be, the prouder she would be of me and then... maybe I'd feel her love!"

There's another Wendy that lives down the street. Her household situation is very similar. Mom is still not particularly warm or nurturing, for her attention is focused on Dad. This Dad is either unavailable mentally, emotionally or physically to Wendy or to Mom. Dad is either at work all the time (workaholic), and/or has a substance abuse of some sort (alcohol, drugs, women, sex, gambling etc.). He continually breaks promises to Mom, Wendy and the rest of the family. Mom and Dad constantly argue. It is Wendy's job to keep the peace, at all costs. She tries to be "perfect" as not to upset her parents any further. She keeps her family life a secret to all her friends, the "perfect picture". Of course perfect it is not. Mom is addicted* to Dad, Dad is addicted to <u>fill in the blank</u> and the rest of the family is being set up for their own areas of dysfunctional coping.

Although the house dynamics might differ somewhat most Wendy's long to escape this constant chaos/drama. She hopes and prays that as we were all taught, "some day my prince will come and I will live happily ever after"!

It's because of the dramas/traumas and dysfunction in the family that Wendy tries desperately to please every one. She is unconsciously setting herself up for a pattern called codependency. Codependency, which in simple terms means – putting others needs/wants in front of your own.

<u>*Addiction</u> – knowing that <u>fill in the blank</u> is not food or healthy for self/others and it continues to cause personal, occupational health, problems, but the conscious use of it continues.

Let's look at co-dependency traits. Do any look familiar?

<u>Compliance Patterns</u>

Co-dependants:
- Compromise their values and integrity to avoid rejection and other people's anger

- Are very sensitive to other's feelings and assume the same feelings
- Are extremely loyal, remaining in harmful situations too long
- Place a higher value on others' opinions and feelings, and are too afraid to express differing viewpoints or feelings
- Accept sex as a substitute for love

Low Self-Esteem Patterns

Codependents:
- have difficulty making decisions,
- judge their thought, words and actions harshly, as never being good enough,
- are embarrassed to receive recognition, praise or gifts,
- are unable to ask others to meet their needs or wants,
- value other people's approval of their thoughts, feelings and behaviors over self-approval.

Denial Patterns

Codependents:
- have difficulty identifying feelings,
- minimize, alter or deny their feelings,
- perceive themselves as being completely unselfish,
- dedicated to the well-being of others.

Control Patterns

Codependents:

- Believe most others are incapable of taking care of themselves,
- Attempt to convince others what they should think and feel,
- Become resentful when others refuse their offers of help,
- Freely offer advice and guidance without being asked,
- Lavish gifts and favors on those they care about,
- Use sex to gain approval and acceptance,
- Have to be needed in order to have a relationship with others

Looking Back . . . Peter

From the day he was born, Peter was the twinkle in his mama's eye. He was simply adored. Even though Dad did not care for the constant attention on Peter, Mom continued to dote on him. Some would say to point of spoiling him. But really, who could resist that impish little boy grin whenever he asked for something? For example, when Peter wanted a toy in the store, he would have a tantrum if mom refused his request. In order not to make a scene in public, Mom would acquiesce.

Unfortunately, unbeknownst to mom, she is rewarding negative behavior and therefore instilling a trait that will remain throughout his adulthood. (i.e. I want – you give – if not – I'll make a scene – throw a tantrum). He usually got his way. Mom was always there for Peter, at home, at school and in the community. He was somewhat troublesome but always blamed others for the incident or situation. Mom would always come to his rescue. She covered up for him and made excuses for him. "He really was such a good little boy." Whatever is permitted...continues. Therefore this behavior pattern continued though out childhood.

Peter's Dad was often unavailable, whether mentally, emotionally, or physically. He just wasn't around very much. If truth were to be told, Peter's Dad never really did want kids. But, it happened anyway. Once the child or children came, there was much less attention paid to Dad. He resented this greatly. He was no longer the center of attention, so often he chose to become unavailable by either leaving permanently or involving himself with work, other women or substance abuses. He was always making promises to Peter, his siblings and to Mom that he couldn't keep. This unavailability from Dad sets up the further closeness between Mom and Peter. Again, whatever is permitted continues. The multigenerational transmission beat goes on . . .

Growing Up?? Or Not!

In normal child development a child goes through a Narcissistic Development Stage, usually beginning around 18 months. It is often referred to as "the terrible twos." In this stage everything revolves around the child himself. The world is his own reflection. Their language is solely ego centered – "I" – "me" "my". He/she is ego centric and ego oriented. Most of us (hopefully) out grow this stage. However, if there is an unusual amount of consistent doting or praise on the child he/she becomes naturally, conditioned to being the center of attention, and therefore, strengthening the ego centered behaviors.

Narcissistic people see the world and see other's behaviors as how it affects them. They sometimes seem cold, or cruel or inconsiderate due to this ego view of existence. But, they can charm those birds straight out of the trees. They walk proudly into a room with that Peter Pan twinkle and boldness and announce "Here I am!" The Peter Pan Syndrome was coined and written by Dr. Dan Kiley. It is said that there are basically two kinds of people in the world – The "Here I ams" and the "There you ares". A Peter, "Here I am!" almost amazingly always finds Wendy whose persona exclaims, "Well, there you are!" The narcissist has an armor of self regard. They often are "braggers". They brag about themselves, their accomplishments or associations. In the Disney movie Peter sings "I gotta crow" and you'll find he's always crowin' about himself! Narcissists cannot handle criticism and seldom think they are incorrect. They have a sense of entitlement, with little or no humility. Mistakes and problems are <u>always</u> blamed on the other person, place or thing. Again, we see this behavior in preschools, "he made me do it", and, in preschool this is normal, but it's not necessarily a great quality in adulthood.

In my opinion, the difference between a child and adult are simply three factors:
1. Accountability;
2. Responsibility for one's actions;
3. Immediate vs. delayed gratification.

A child wants what he wants what he wants <u>now</u>. A child does what they <u>want</u> to do. An Adult does what he <u>needs</u> to do. Wouldn't we all like to stay in bed and watch T.V. cartoons all morning? Sure, but we <u>need</u> to go to work. We <u>need</u> to be responsible and accountable to maturely delay our desire for instant gratification. An adult realizes he cannot always have what he desires immediately. We must wait, most times, for the rewards of life and living. So when we say that someone is immature, I feel it means that they have not mastered these three steps needed for a <u>mature</u> adult.

The narcissist needs to be the center of attention and has a very strong, but "false" ego. They are consciously or unconsciously fearful that someone will discover their "real self". And that they are in fact not all they pretend to be. The fear they will be unveiled. A great example of false ego is the "Wiz" in the Wizard of Oz. In the end, we discover, The Wiz is only a man not the great Wizard of Oz with special powers we imagined or were lead to believe.

Do we all have that fear of being "found out"? I tend to think we all wear "masks." A mask is our "real" self versus our "ideal" self. Our masks hide the innate fear in all of us. We think, "maybe if they really knew what I was really like they wouldn't like me, and then they would reject me or abandon me". Let's be honest we are all different with different people, different surroundings and situations. The real self is described as who we really are. The "ideal" self is the self projected into who we think we should be, or who we or others want us to be. The "Imposter Syndrome" is described as feelings of self doubt, vulnerability, lack of self confidence. (Theimpostersyndrome. com). The more incongruent the "real" self is from the "ideal" self, the deeper the loss of the authentic being. The goal then for most of us to be authentic . . . to be who we truly are and accept ourselves as just that! Sounds really simple doesn't it??

<u>Masks</u>

Don't be fooled by the face I wear, for I wear a
thousand masks.
And none of them are me.
Don't be fooled, for God's sake, don't be fooled.
I give you the impression that I'm secure, that
confidence is my
Name and coolness is my game,
And that I need no one. But don't believe me.
Beneath dwells the real me in confusion, in
aloneness, in fear.
That's why I create a mask to hide behind, to
shield me from the
Glance that knows,
But such a glance is precisely my salvation.
That is, if it's followed by acceptance, if it's
followed by love.
It's the only thing that can liberate me from my
own self-built prison walls.
I'm afraid that deep down I'm nothing and that
I'm just no good. And that you will reject me.

Please listen carefully and try to hear what
I'm not saying. I'd really like to be genuine and
spontaneous, and me. But you've got to help me.
You've got to hold out your hand.
Each time you're kind and gentle, and
encouraging Each time you try to understand
because you really care.
My heart begins to grow wings, feeble wings, but
wings.
With your sensitivity and sympathy, and your
power of understanding.
You alone can release me from my shallow world
of uncertainty.
It will not be easy for you. The nearer you
approach me. The blinder I may strike back.
But I'm told that Love is stronger than strong
walls,
And in this lies my only hope. Please try to beat
down the walls with firm hands,
But gentle hands, for a child is very sensitive.
Who am I, you may wonder.
I am every man you meet, and also every woman
that you meet.And I am you, also.

Author unknown
(adapted from "Please Hear What I'm Not Saying")

The Mother And Child Reunion

Back to our couple. The first few months with Wendy's new beau seem to be going fairly well. Her Peter is charming, unpredictable and always wanting to have fun. He really enjoys life and has lots of fun friends. There seems to be a childlike aura around him. People seem to be drawn to him like a magnet, for he IS most entertaining. Wendy is also enjoying this "muse". She feels like she is beginning to come out of her "responsible-reliable" shell. She still is concerned about his drinking a little too much on occasion and that his jobs seem to "come and go", because he says, "his bosses are always stupid." (He reminds her, in a strange way, of her Dad.) He borrows money from her with the promise of "I'll pay ya right back", but it doesn't seem to happen. She notices other things. He doesn't always call when he says he will or call when he is going to be late. He always finds an excuse and it is always the other guys fault ("my buddy's car broke down" etc.) She feels that he says one thing and does another. He manipulates. Wendy doesn't understand this. It is almost as if she cannot trust him a great deal of the time. He seems to have good intentions, but he just doesn't seem to follow through! He breaks promises. He always says "I'll get around to it". She feels she is constantly scolding Peter and she is beginning to feel like his mother! (And Peter the disobedient child.) She is constantly nagging, reminding and begging him to fulfill his intentions. He yells,

"Don't criticize me! You're treating me like a child and I won't have it! I can come and go where ever and when ever I want and with whom I want and I don't need your approval- got that?" He is a master at manipulation and passive – aggressive behaviors in order to get his needs met. Then later, he might soften and apologize. He tells Wendy, "I promise to be better, tomorrow" etc. Remember he NEEDS her stability. He makes more excuses (and she in turn makes excuses for his behavior to herself and others.) But then again, with Peter's charm, he convinces Wendy with his twinkling eyes that "this will be the last time" etc. and…that magical spell he has on her resumes. She trusts once more. "Maybe this time", she thinks.

Now we have established that Peter needs Wendy. (Not that his ego would ever admit that!) But indeed he needs her stability and her responsible life. She makes most of the money, she pays the bills, she takes care of both of them! She feeds his hungry, never satisfied ego, and nurtures him. He is certainly not "commitment phobic." Quite to the contrary, he wants to be connected. In the Disney movie, when Peters "shadow" playfully eludes him, it was Wendy who sewed his shadow back on for him! (codependent) According to Jung, the shadow describes the part of the psyche that an individual would rather not acknowledge. It contains the denied parts of the self. A healthy psyche, however comes from having accepted your shadow parts and integrated them as components of yourself.

In the movie, after the sewing was complete, Peter jumps up with a huge grin and exclaims "Ah, the cleverness of <u>me</u>!" Also, in the movie, isn't it amazing that Peter always lands on his feet! (Now is that little tidbit fact or fiction?) So we ask why does Wendy need Peter? I ask my Wendy's this question in our therapy sessions and these are some of the replies, "If he leaves, I'll be alone and I can't handle that." "I know I make more money and that I take care of everything, but he does help, sometimes and I don't like being by myself or going out to the bars or wherever to look for someone better." "You know most men are jerks and I just don't want to start over." Another Wendy states, "I know he's immature and undependable, but he needs me and he really does have his good days!"

But there is another reason that Wendy stays... <u>her own ego</u>! My Wendy's tell me that her Peter feeds her ego because she knows that she is smarter and more capable, Also she knows that he really needs her, more than she needs him! She knows she is in control. After her chaotic childhood, she now has a sense of control. And that helps her self esteem. Because mentally, emotionally, physically and financially he is more dependant on her! And, she knows that! So the "hook" goes both ways!

Women's liberation got women out of the kitchen and into the boardroom. They have many more choices and are free to make decisions today that they could never have made years ago. Women are finding successful careers as never before. College Campuses are now statistically over 53% female and men are often intimidated by successful women. Many very successful career women find themselves very lonely, and many times, they will to find "Peters," just so they won't be alone every Saturday night. Well, that sure does work for Peter, doesn't it??? Whoopee, he's found the buried treasure! So the hook up works for both of them and the Mother and Child reunion is only a heart break away . . .

The Addiction Triangle

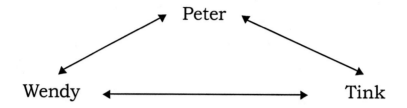

As presented previously, the meaning of addiction is simply: "knowing that <u>fill in the blank,</u> is not good or healthy for me, mentally, physically, emotionally, spiritually or financially but, I continue to use."

Whether the "blank" is relationships, work, food, exercise, drugs, alcohol, sex, porno, shopping, gambling, etc. it doesn't matter, for they are all basically the same. When we consciously choose negatives for our lives and <u>continue</u> to use them..... we are addicted.

We have already established that Wendy is hooked or addicted to Peter. She hopes, he will change but deep inside her head, she knows the odds are poor. She knows he is not healthy for her and she is unhappy a great deal of the time but she feels if she leaves, she has lost her purpose of being "needed." And worse than that, she'd be <u>lonely</u> and alone again. Her fear of loneliness and abandonment keep her addiction strong. Wendy's tell me, "I know that the relationship is rocky, but everyone has their problems and besides, when he's being 'good' (like a child) it is great but when he's 'bad' . . . it's pretty awful and besides, I don't want to be alone".

We have also established that Peter is hooked/addicted to Wendy. He needs to be advised, taken care of and he needs her stability (especially financially). Wendy takes care of the bills, the household and allows him go out with his friends the ("Lost boys"). He hates her "nagging", but he doesn't think any of it is his fault. (Is <u>any</u> thing ever Peter's fault?)

But, Peter has another addiction. He is almost always addicted to "Tink". In the book, Tinkerbell is the impish little fairy that whispers naughty messages into Peter's ear. In reality, I feel, "Tink" is Peter's addiction nature. That often is manifested in drugs, alcohol, sex (porno) other relationships, gambling, food etc. Tink tells Peter to "go ahead, who cares if Wendy gets mad at you?" Peter indulges, but not without fencing with a "Captain Hook". His adult conscious is trying to hook him into being responsible, doing what he should do and not what he wants to do (child vs Adult). He has a mental struggle with his enemy, fighting with the destructive force of the addiction. The battle is sometimes fierce, but usually Peter wins, the Hook gives in and Tink....gets her way. Tada!

Wendy hates Tink and visa versa. She feels Tink is at the center of all their problems.

In fact, "Tink" is a very big problem, but not the core. Perhaps Peters charm and finesse can convince Wendy that he is finished with Tink. Wendy is doubtful, but again, acquiesces and falls back under Peter's magical spell once more. IF Peter can break his current addiction(s), it is usually emotionally or physically replaced by another one. IF Wendy can replace her addiction, she often finds another Peter – replacement.

The multi generational cyclical (sick-li-cal) circle of addiction continues.

Never Never Never Neverland!

In the story, Peter Pan comes magically into Wendy's life through and open window. (What a metaphor, could she be lonely and/or vulnerable? Nah!)

Peter teaches her to "think happy thoughts and with faith, trust and Pixie dust, you can fly." The exhilaration of freedom has never happened to her before! Then he tells her about a place where she will never, ever have to grow up! She becomes seduced by Peter and throws her responsible, dependable self "out the window" and Wendy flies away with him. She lands in a place where there are no rules – just unruly lost boys who need a mother. They have no responsibility, no discipline, and they vow that they never will and never want to grow up!

Wendy finds herself having to be the responsible adult. The freedom she initially felt is gone. She will never, never, never be able to be truly free and childlike (like Peter promised) she feels abandoned because he was supposed to be her knight in shining armor/her savior from loneliness.

Now with due respect to Sir Barrie, why would any one go to a place like this?? The answer is because <u>it wasn't supposed to be like this</u> – Peter <u>promised</u> magic!

But the "magic" quickly begins to fade. Wendy feels betrayed and Peter becomes annoyed because he feels she has lost her joyful spirit and does not join in his merriment.

Does any of this sound familiar? Unfortunately, Sir Barrie's metaphor is so painfully similar to so many of our own lives. If someone gives us promises that they either can't or won't deliver or honor we feel betrayed and angry.

The roots of anger are feelings of hurt, fear, abandonment, rejection, and betrayal (guilt and shame feelings often co-exist). Anger when escalated outward turns to rage (or feeling out of control) which often has tragic consequences (as we see in domestic violence situations). Anger if repressed, or turned inward, becomes <u>depression</u>.

<u>Anger outwardly expressed</u> → <u>Rage</u>.

<u>Anger</u> → <u>Fire</u> → Rage → out of control

Hurt Fear
Abandonment
Betrayal   match
Rejection
Guilt/Shame

<u>Anger inwardly expressed</u> →   <u>Depression</u>

As one might already know, the origin of these feelings begins in childhood. Often, we fear that expressing painful feelings (anger) can lead to <u>rejection or abandonment</u> by our caregivers and therefore the loss of our love attachment.

What then, does this young child do with these feelings that are just normal for all of us? He/she has no choice but to deny them, get out the aggression or stuff them deep inside, like a secret. The family laws become, "Don't talk, don't tell, don't feel" and don't rock the boat."

But often as we know, these stuffed feeling, manifest themselves physically, mentally or emotionally and are very painful. As a child, there seems to be no "escape", but many quickly learn there is <u>relief</u>. The relief may be temporary, but it eases the pain.

In my practice, I use the following metaphor. I call it "food poisoning" (it is <u>feeling</u> poison). We learn to go to the medicine cabinet for relief and choose the "bottle" that works for us. They all come in various shapes and sizes, but all have basically the same ingredient – relief from the pain. The bottle might be labeled work food, shopping, drugs, alcohol, gambling, sex/sexual addictions and/or <u>relationships</u>. They all can be additive and addictions always escalate and therefore, can become extremely dangerous and /or life altering.

<u>The Addiction Cycle</u>

Pain – medicine cabinet – choose bottle of choice for (temporary) relief – pain returns → "bottle → habit → addiction → cycle continues.

Wendy's "drug of choice" is Peter. The toxic effects of the substance, escalates and begins to backfire. As with all addictions the "highs" become less, the lows become more. She is beginning to realize that Never, Never, Never Land has no solid ground – just promises and pixie dust.

She is finding the addiction to Peter is becoming exhausting and frustrating. She is very unhappy, miserable in fact, but her fear of being ALONE, prevents her from detachment and detoxing.

In sessions, each Wendy tells me the same sentence, "I don't want to be alone again". I tell them to see the real reality of the situation and to cognitively realize that they are already alone! Peter is not reliable, responsible or accountable. She cannot consistently trust him and without trust, there is no relationship with anyone – friend, mate, family member, employer, employee, pet, etc.

I feel that facing the fear of being alone is far better, than the fear of being unhappy, trapped, self sabotaging and addicted.

Wendy feels abandoned by Peter, but in fact, far worse, she has abandoned herself, her identity and sense of self. She has allowed her self esteem, self regard, and spirit to become manipulated and wounded. She has allowed herself to become a victim in another's agenda, not her own. She is tired of the struggle and the battle and tired of the constant drama, trauma and chaos. (Her childhood repeats itself.)

Wendy has two choices: to stay or to leave – both take courage. But, I feel it takes much more courage to let go, than to hold on to the pain and abuse. The decision will always be hers, because our Peter doesn't make decisions and also in reality, he needs her more than she needs him.

If Wendy does make the decision to detox, and work toward recovery, she has taken the first brave step toward regaining her self respect and sense of self. The decision to detach and the process, is extremely difficult and painful. It is similar to a death.

Wendy's (denial) cannot believe the relationship is dying. She misses him terribly, she cries constantly, she feels she cannot bear the loss of Peter. The emotions are constant and deeply devastating (anger). She rationalizes, she ruminates (bargaining) and she is deeply depressed.

The process of grief/loss occurs. The stages are denial, anger, bargaining, depression and acceptance.

Denial – initial shock, disbelief, numbness.

Anger – hurt, fear, abandonment, rejection, betrayal.

Bargaining – back and forth, rehearsal of guilt, shame, anguish.

Depression – anger turned inward.

Acceptance – acquiesce, consent, yield to reality.

But Wendy must realize that she has become emotionally, mentally, physically, financially and most important spiritually wounded. She cannot begin to pursue her own dreams and goals with some one else tethered to her feet. She <u>must</u> cut the cord.

Wendy knows she wants to be in a healthy relationship but she tells me, "I have never been in one and I don't have a clue <u>what</u> healthy relationship is!"

Wendy again, vacillates between going back (habit) or going forward (risk) but she begins to understand that if she continues down the same street she will continue to fall in the same hole . . . again . . . and again . . .

Autobiography In Five Chapters

Chapter I

I walk down the street.

There is a deep hole in the sidewalk.

I fall in.

I am lost...I am helpless---it isn't my fault

It takes forever to find a way out.

Chapter II

I walk down the same street.

There is a deep hole in the sidewalk.

I pretend I don't see it.

I fall in again.

I can't believe I am in the same place – but it isn't my fault.

It still takes a long time to get out.

Chapter III

I walk down the same street.

There is a deep hole in the sidewalk.

I see it is here.

I still fall in...it's a habit.

My eyes are open, I know where I am.

It is my fault.

I climb out immediately.

Chapter IV

I walk down the same street.

There is a deep hole in the sidewalk.

I walk around it.

Chapter V

I walk down another street.

Unknown author

A.K.A.
(If I keep on doing what I'm doing – I'll keep getting what I got.)

Giving up doesn't always mean you
Are weak
Sometimes it means that you are
strong enough to let go.

"Let Go"

To "let go" does not mean to stop caring.
It means I can't do it for someone else.

To "let go" is not to cut myself off.
It's the realization I can't control another.

To "let go" is not to enable,
but to allow learning from natural
consequences.

To "let go" is to admit powerlessness
which means the outcome is not in my hands.

To "let go" is not to try to change or blame
another,
It's to make the most of myself.

To "let go" is not to care for,
but to care about.

To "let go" is not to fix, but to be supportive.

To "let go" is not to judge,
but to allow another to be a human being.

To "let go" is not to be in the middle arranging
all the outcomes,
but to allow other to affect their destinies.

To "let go" is not to be protective.
It's to permit another to face reality.

To "let go" is not to deny, but to accept.

To "let go" is not to nag, scold or argue
but instead to search out my own
shortcomings
and correct them.

To "let go" is not to adjust everything to my
desires, but to take each day as it comes and
cherish myself in it.

To "let go" is not to criticize and regulate
anybody, but to try to become what I dream I
can be.

To "let go" is not to regret the past, but to
grow and live for the future.
To "let go" is to fear less and LOVE MORE.

Healthy Relationship

Just what IS a healthy relationship? Most of us have been in unhealthy relationships for so long, that we don't have a clue as to what constitutes a healthy one! Perhaps we have been or are in unhealthy relationships with our parents, siblings, mates, children, friends, bosses, employers, employees, etc. etc. for so long, it almost seems normal. We simply become stuck in our habits or patterns with ourselves and/or with others. We know they are not healthy, but they continue. We <u>tolerate</u> the "normal dysfunctional" relationship. And often repeat the same rules and roles of our family of origin.

I feel the reason we are in unhealthy relationships is due to the factor that we all are uncomfortable with change, real honesty and confrontation. We remain in these relationships because we feel it is easier (which it is not). We rationalize to ourselves "they will never change, so why bother?" We minimize, "that is just the way they are." Perhaps these relationships are hurtful, abusive or even life threatening. But we stay in them due to our fear. We fear change (or something new) so we remain stuck and continue to repeat the same patterns with no positive results.

We think, "Oh if they would only change, I wouldn't be so miserable." We work very hard trying to change others but, they do not change.

Therefore our efforts are futile and we continue to be unhappy. So what do we do??

Begin to heal-thy-SELF !! And this little prayer says it all...

God grant me the serenity to accept the people I cannot change, have the courage to change the only one I can, and the wisdom to know...that it's ME.

We truly cannot change anyone but ourselves. If you wait for someone else to make you happy, you will wait forever. Contrary to some beliefs, no one can make you happy or a whole person but you!. You have two choices. You can choose to accept others, as they are, or you can choose to walk away. Remember, if you need to change someone, you are in the wrong relationship.

Again a healthy relationship with ANY one begins with mutual trust and mutual respect. This is the cement of a relationship. Trust and respect for ourselves first, for with out consistent trust and respect there simply is no self or relationship. It is not negotiable nor can it be compromised – bottom line. People are afraid to be honest with one another. We are all vulnerable and fear showing ones "shadow side". We fear being honest with another could cause rejection. Therefore we end up with assumptions and mind games. We do not like confrontation. It is often very uncomfortable, so we just remain silent with our feelings and thoughts. A healthy relationship is authentic, honest and open, not false and pretending.

A healthy relationship makes us <u>better</u>! It is the cherry on top of the hot fudge sundae. The sundae is wonderful, and complete by itself. The cherry just makes it better! A good relationship makes us <u>HAPPY</u> not depressed or sad. There are no good days verses bad days. It is consistent. No relationship is perfect, but 98% of the time a healthy relationship is stable, equal and loving.

I feel there are three factors that constitute a healthy love relationship—"Like", love and "in love". You can like someone and love someone (like a good friend), but not be in love with them. You can love someone without liking them etc. etc. However, all three elements must be present, on a consistent basis, in order to have a long, lasting, healthy relationship. First, you need to truly like the person, respect them and enjoy their spirit. Second you need to love them, despite their short comings (which we all have) and third, having <u>that</u> feeling, that <u>magic</u>, is crucial at the beginning. It is the flash, the spark that ignites the fire. I have found that couples who initially did not have this important quality, have difficulty down the path. As will all fires, the spark transfers to crackling flames, then the hottest part of the fire, the embers, are the lasting depth of the process. Continuing with the metaphor, the fire must occasionally refueled and stoked to be kept alive.

Ask yourself, is my relationship (with _____ _____) healthy? Is there consistent trust, respect, honesty, and open communication? Is there a good balance?

Some couples have what I call a "90/10" – one partner gives 90%, the other 10%. The balance should be 40/60 – 60/40 give and take, compromise negotiation and honest communication.

Again, always remember, living with anyone requires compromise. I call the compromise, "marble fudge": i.e. "He wants chocolate, I want vanilla and we can order only one dessert – what do we do? The solution is, marble fudge – (chocolate chip or Neapolitan) – then both partners get some of what they want. It is a win – win for each one. It takes work, creativity, and flexibility and a true desire to strive for that healthy balance and compromise. Sometimes, I feel the true meaning of love is doing something for someone that you don't want to do. For example, he hates the ballet, but he surprises her with tickets (and a smile) because she loves the ballet! It is easy to do something for someone when we want to and we obtain pleasure also. But, to give 100% to someone, when we don't get anything out of it but their delight and pleasure, now that is true love (sigh). But, here again, there must be a mutual balance (she has to "lovingly endure" the boxing match!)

A healthy relationship must also have a healthy balance: mentally, physically, emotionally and spiritually. Many people think, "our two halves make us whole" – wrong. Two halves are simply that. Two whole, balanced people make a whole.

Two healthy people treat each other kindly. We are often nicer to the butcher than we are to our own mate. Compliments, little notes, just being thoughtful all these are crucial to "the fire". This should be a joyful daily process, for both partners. (After all, aren't you supposed to be in a relationship with someone you like, love and are in love with?)

A healthy relationship cannot survive with out a good, hearty, healthy <u>sense</u> of <u>humor</u>! Life is full of challenges and rough roads, if a couple cannot learn to grow and laugh through some of these, they are in deep trouble.

Also a rich spiritual connection – faith and hope in a higher power can produce miracles and bring couples through many a storm.

But, the ultimate ingredient is in TIME. I ask my couples at each initial session, "How much time do you spend together?" The look is puzzlement and the answer is <u>always</u> the same, "with just each other?" I chuckle, "yes, with just each other." Their response is "not very much, in fact, can't remember the last time."

Couples tell me, they "just run out of time – with the jobs, the kids, and their activities etc.

etc." But what happen down the road, when the kids are gone and the kids were the glue? Then probably the couple's empty nest falls apart. The couple are now strangers.

Time scheduling is difficult for all of us in these hectic times. However, if it is to be a healthy relationship, a couple <u>must</u> consistently <u>take</u> the time. They must <u>make</u> the time to be together – to nourish and enrich each other in their relationship. Many schedule a date night once a week, even if it's just special time at home together. Yes, just the two of you. Feed the children early and enjoy candlelight, conversation and each other. It is a choice, to exercise the marriage muscle or, let it atrophy. They say, anything worth while takes time and effort and a healthy relationship is a strong, toned muscle.

Leaving The Clubhouse And Learning To Fly (Or Life Begins When You Get One!)

Recovering from any addiction is a long and difficult process. It is a daily decision and one based on our own admitted helplessness and our will and determination to become dependant – free and heal - thy (mentally, physically, emotionally and spiritually) self. But more importantly, the decision to recover and discover the inner treasure of yourself is to be able to have the self regard to regain your own identity. Remember, you have learned and grown through this journey. You are now stronger, better (not bitter) and the best is yet to come on your future path.

This process will need outside support and guidance from a source other than family or friends. I feel they are often too close to be able to provide good perspective and healthy advice.

I suggest a spiritual mentor, a licensed therapist with special expertise in this area, and/or a 12 step program such as Codependent Anonymous (CODA). Individual guidance and group support is an excellent combination.

Together, they can assist with the grief/loss phase and the transformation phase, in a healthy manner. Remember you do have a <u>choice</u> and it does require change, which is difficult for all of us. (A change in hair style or color is hard enough, let alone individual lifestyle change.)

Awareness, plus honest assessment is needed, if your lifestyle is to promote change. If you are aware of your unhealthy patterns, then, honestly assess your role in it, and make the decision to change the pattern, you are ready to begin to learn to fly! Perhaps, you finally realized that you already have been flying solo in the relationship for a long time. There will be a temporary loneliness (that is why you need professional support) but it will be overwhelmed by the new found peace and serenity in your life. There is risk, of course. Life is a daily risk, but no risk, no growth, no pain --- no gain! Growth is knowing you have a choice! Growing up is choosing for ourselves. (In Wendy's case, only when she decides to trust and depend on herself, can she truly grow up and "fly.")

Growth requires a change in our thinking and our behaviors. A low opinion of ourselves and a low sense of self regard and self esteem are usually seeded when we were young and we continue to foster the false belief. We continue to think negatively, and think we are not "good enough". (The inner child questioning ourselves) It is no surprise that we therefore end up in relationships that foster our same negative thinking. Because of our low sense of ourselves, we have no believable defense. So when someone blames us for a situation or points the finger at us, we then feed the tumor of low self esteem by believing them! We listen to others not ourselves. Often people with a false ego will blame others to enhance their own esteem. They then feel better about themselves, and we feel worse about ourselves. We then begin to falsely believe that they must be right and we are wrong, i.e. "It must be me".

Those negative thoughts continue to feed our low self esteem. Only when we begin to assess and examine this self abusive and ridiculous pattern, can we see this cycle and choose to break it.

We did not have a choice as children. If we were hurt or abused mentally, physically or emotionally we had no way out. But, we are "grownups" now and we can choose our own mental messages to our selves! We can change the self sabotaging negatives tapes and replace them with positive, self supportive encouraging tapes. (Reverse the negative inner critic) We can rehearse and memorize them and slowly, but surely, begin to believe them. "I am a good person. I am proud of myself. I deserve respect and dignity from others. I like who I am. I love the child that is me and I love the adult that I am." (That connection is critical). Why are we worrying about others opinions of us? It is our opinion of ourselves that matters, you will never have a healthy self esteem if you listen to others, instead of your self. Be your own self and be proud of you! Remember about all you can do in life is be yourself. Some people will love you for you. Most will love you for what you can do for THEM and, some will not like you at all.

Dare to dream – dare to visualize.

As an adult you can now <u>choose</u> to change the colors in your paint box, to paint <u>your</u> life. As children we could not choose. We were stuck with the colors that were chosen for us. If you look at your life and those original colors are not working for you today – <u>TAKE</u> <u>THEM</u> <u>OUT</u>. Replace them with the new colors that <u>you</u> choose! Choice – risk – growth – peace – power. Paint your own life picture with our own choice of colors, patterns and talents. Don't let anyone paint your picture or choose your colors for you. If you choose to <u>let</u> them, it is NOT your painting. You have the choice.

Once you understand and internalize this concept, your world will begin to change and evolve and transform. It is the meaning, message, and lessons of our lives journey, to learn from our past, with all it's pain and challenges, and grow forward <u>because</u> <u>of</u> <u>them</u>. Our challenges and struggles are the builders of our character and our integrity. (Oprah – "Our past is our strength")

Scott Peck presents this brilliant thought:

"To proceed through the desert you must be able to meet existential suffering and work it through. In order to do that you must change your attitude toward pain, in one way or another. The quickest way to do that, and here's the good news- is to realize that <u>everything</u> that happens to us has been designed for our spiritual growth." Scott Peck, *The Road Less Traveled.*

(Again, no pain – no gain- no risk – no growth.)

Don't choose to continue your own family patterns of dysfunction – past or present. Perhaps we were handed "baggage" which was generational and continues to be handed down today. It is up to You to discard the old baggage that is damaged and break those unhealthy patterns of the past, set new goals for your life, and to choose to <u>grow forward</u>.

We do not grow from the "easy times". Growth comes from the challenge, the struggles and only then, can come the victory and pride of accomplishment. (Only when it's dark can you see the stars).

The lessons from the journey must be savored and also passed forward. As your candle becomes lit, it is your opportunity to be there for someone behind you. Because of your pain and therefore, growth, you can now teach and light the candle for someone else. The illumination can lead generations out of the darkness. Reach up to your higher power and reach out to others and reach in to your true self. In order to fly, you <u>must</u> trust and believe in yourself. Only that wonderful sense of self pride can propel your journey and give you wings.

Believe in yourself, believe in your spirit, spirituality, your purpose, your power, your ideals and your joyful metamorphosis and transformation.

Remember, think these "happy thoughts" for they will always lift you up. Believe in you, believe in <u>your</u> magic. You will then have the strength and spirit to walk out that Clubhouse door, fly and . . . truly . . . begin to soar!

The End?
No, Just the beginning . . . . . .

When you have reached the end of all the light
that you know and you must step out into the
darkness of the unknown,
Faith is knowing that one of two things will
happen:
Either you will have something solid to stand on
or you will be taught how to fly!

Author unknown

<u>Inspirations And Life 101</u>
<u>Exam: Life 101</u>

What have I learned
From this experience?
How have I grown?
How am I the same?
How am I different?
What has the pain
taught me?
How will I live my life
differently <u>because</u> of
this experience?
How can I make a difference
For others because of my lessons
and growth?

<u>Prayer For Serenity</u>

God grant me the serenity to
accept the things I cannot change,
the courage to change the things I can.
And the wisdom to know the difference.
Living one day at a time, Enjoying hardship as a
pathway to peace;
taking, as Jesus did this sinful world as it is. Not
as I would have it;
trusting that You will make all things right If I
surrender to your will;
so that I may be reasonably happy in the life and
supremely happy with You forever in the next.
Amen

Reinhold Niebuhr

And then the day came when
The risk to remain tight in a
Bud was more painful than the
Risk it took to blossom

The Weaver

"But then shall I know even as also I am known"
(1 Cor. 13:12)

My life is but a weaving between my Lord and
me, I cannot choose the colors he worketh
steadidly.
Oftimes He weaveth sorrow, and I, in foolish
pride forget he sees the upper,
and I, the under side. Not till the loom is silent
and the shuttles cease to fly shall God unroll the
canvas
and explain the reason why.
The dark threads are as needful
in the Weaver's skillful hand
as the threads of gold and silver
in the pattern He has planned.

After Awhile

After awhile you learn the subtle difference
between holding a hand and chaining a soul.
And you learn that love doesn't mean leaning.
And company doesn't mean security. And you
begin to learn that kisses aren't contracts and
presents aren't promises.
And you begin to accept your defeats with your
head up and your eyes ahead, with the grace of
a man not the grief of a child. And you learn to
build all your roads on today because
tomorrow's ground is too uncertain for plans and
futures have a way of falling down in mid-flight.
After awhile you learn that even sunshine burns
if you ask too much.
So you plant your garden and decorate your own
soul, instead of waiting for someone to bring you
flowers.
And you learn that you really can endure, that
you really are strong, and you really do have
worth.

And you learn with every good-bye you learn.

Author unknown

Don't Look Back

Author: Unknown
As you travel through life there are
always those times, when decisions just have to
be made...
when the choices are hard and the solutions
seem scarce...
...and the rain seems to soak your parade
There are some situations where all you can do
is to simply let go and move on...
...gather courage together and choose a direction
that carries you toward a new dawn.
So pack up your troubles and take a step
forward-----
The process of change can be tough...
...but think about all the excitement ahead if you
can be stalwart enough!
There can be adventures you never imagined just
awaiting around the bend...
...and wishes and dreams just about to come
true in ways you can't yet comprehend!

Perhaps you'll find friendships that spring from
new interests as you challenge your status quo...
...and learn there are so many options in life,
and so many ways you can grow!
Perhaps new places you never expected to see
things you've never seen...
...or travel to fabulous, faraway worlds and
wonderful spots in between!
Perhaps you'll find warmth and affection and
caring...
a "somebody special" who's there...
...to help you stay centered and listen with
interest to stories and feelings you share.
Perhaps you'll find comfort in knowing your
friends are supportive of all that you do...
...and believe that whatever decisions you make,
they'll be the right choices for you!
So keep putting one foot in front of the other...
...taking your life day by day.
There's a brighter tomorrow that's just down the
road.
Don't look back you're not going that way!

__The Promise__

Promise yourself to be so strong that nothing can disturb your peace of mind. To talk health, happiness and prosperity to every person you meet. To make all your friends feel that there is something in them. To look only at the sunny side of everything and make your optimism come true. To think only the best, to work for only for the best, and expect only the best. To be just as enthusiastic about the success of others as you are of your own. To forget the mistakes of the past, and press on to the greater achievements of the future. To wear a cheerful countenance at all times and give every living creature you meet a smile. To give so much time to the improvement of yourself that you have no time to criticize others. To be too large to worry, too noble for anger, too strong for fear and too happy to permit the presence of trouble.

Just For Today

1. Just for today I will try to live through this day only, not to tackle my whole life problem at once. I can do things for 12 hours that would appall me if I had to keep them for a lifetime.

2. Just for today I will be happy. This assumes that what Abraham Lincoln said is true, that "most folks are about as happy as the make up their minds to be." Happiness is from within; it is not a matter of externals.

3. Just for today I will try to adjust myself to what is, and not try to adjust everything to my own desires. I will take my family, my business, and my licks as they come and fit myself to them.

4. Just for today I will take care of my body. I will exercise it, care for it, nourish it, not abuse or neglect it, so that it will be a perfect machine for my bidding.

5. Just for today, I will try to strengthen my mind. I will learn something useful. I will not be

a mental loafer. I will read something that requires effort, thought and concentration.

6. Just for today I will exercise my soul in three ways; I will do somebody a good turn and not get found out; I will do at least two things I don't want to do as William James suggests, just for exercise.

7. Just for today I will be agreeable. I will look as well as I can, dress becomingly as possible, talk low, act courteously, be liberal with praise, criticize not at all, nor find fault with anything and <u>not try to regulate or</u> <u>improve anyone</u>.

8. Just for today I will have a program. I will write down what I expect to do every hour. I may not follow it exactly, but I will have it. It will eliminate two pests – hurry and indecision.

9. Just for today I will have a quiet half hour all by myself and relax. In this half hour sometimes I will thank God, so as to get a little more perspective to my life.

10. Just for today I will be unafraid, especially I will not be afraid to be happy, to enjoy what is beautiful, to love, and to believe that those I love, love me.

Those who have known a problem first hand
Are usually better able to help others walking
Through the same difficulty

The difference between
Stumbling blocks and stepping stones
Is the way we use them

That Was Then . . . . . . This Is Now!!!!!!!

Everyone we meet teaches us lessons....
People come into your life for a reason, a season
or a lifetime.

When you know which one it is, you will know
what to do for that person. When someone is in
your life for a **REASON**, it is usually to meet a
need you have expressed.
They have come to assist you through difficulty,
to provide you with guidance and support, to aid
you physically, emotionally or spiritually. They
may seem like a Godsend and they are. They are
there for the reason you need them to be.
Then, without any wrongdoing on your part or at
an inconvenient time, this person will say or do
something to bring the relationship to an end.
Sometimes they die. Sometimes they walk away.
Sometimes they act up and force you to take a

stand. What we must realize is that our need has been met, our desire fulfilled, their work is done. The prayer you sent up has been answered and now it is time to move on.

Some people come into your life for a **SEASON**, because your Turn has come to share, grow, or learn. They bring you an experience of peace or make you laugh. They may teach you something you have never done. They usually give you an unbelievable amount of joy.

LIFETIME relationships teach you lifetime lessons, things you must build upon in order to have a solid foundation. Your job is to accept the lesson, love the person and put what you have learned to use in all other relationships and areas of your life.

It is said that love is blind, but friendship is clairvoyant.
Thank you for being a part of my life, whether you were a reason, or a season.

Affirmations That Make Life Work

Say five times in the morning and five times at night (whether you believe them or not).

1. I like myself unconditionally and I enjoy being the unique person that I am.
2. I have ample leisure time and deserve to find, create and feel joy.
3. I am a fallible human being, who makes mistakes.
4. I am a worth-while and lovable human being.
5. I am completely self-determined and I give others that same right.
6. I am a unique and precious human being... doing the best I can, growing in wisdom and love.
7. I am in charge of my own life.
8. My #1 responsibility is my own growth and well-being. The better I am to me, the better I will be to others.

9. I make my own decisions and assume responsibility of any consequences.

10. I am not my actions. I am the actor. My actions may be good or bad. That doesn't make me good or bad.

11. I do not have to prove myself to anyone. I need only to express myself as honestly and effectively as I am capable.

12. My emotional well being is dependent primarily on how I love me.

13. I am kind and gentle towards me.

14. I live a day at a time, do first things first.

15. I am patient and serene for I have the rest of my life in which to grow.

16. Every experience I have in life (even the unpleasant ones) contributes to my learning and growth.

17. No one in the world is more important that I as a person.

18. I have a right to take my space in this world.

19. I am enough.

20. I am loyal, forgiving and gentle to me.

21. I now choose to love, to accept, to embrace and to fully appreciate myself unconditionally.

22. I create my reality.

23. I have a Higher Power who loves me unconditionally.

People come into your life
for a reason, a season
or a lifetime.

Learn from the past and look to the future, but
Master the present.

"Life isn't measured by the breaths you take, but
by
the moments that take your breath away".

Anonymous

The Light of God surrounds me.
The Love of God enfolds me.
The Power of God protects me.
The presence of God watches over me.
Wherever I am, God is.

Today may there be peace within you. May you trust God that you are exactly where you are meant to be. May you use those gifts that you have received, and pass on the love that has been given to you. May you be content knowing that you are a child of God. Let his presence settle into your bones, and allow your soul the freedom to sing, dance, and to bask in the sun. It is there for each and every one of you.

WHAT YOU THINK, YOU CREATE

WHAT YOU FEEL, YOU ATTRACT

WHAT YOU IMAGINE, YOU BECOME...

Adele Basheer

THE MAGICAL METAMORPHSIS

From the struggle of the cocoon
  To the magic and beauty of the butterfly
These now are yours
  As you begin to spread your wings and soar...

Patricia Craine

Life time friends
Suzanne Foley
Tom Ingent
Ginny + Jack
Kathy Miller
Joanne McNamara
Virgil
Barbara Season
Jim Tompkins
George + Helen (season)
Ellie

Printed in the United States
80725LV00002B/202-279